100 Days on Earth

JOHNATHAN J. AZAR

Cover illustrated by John Mungiello

ISBN: 9781076658708

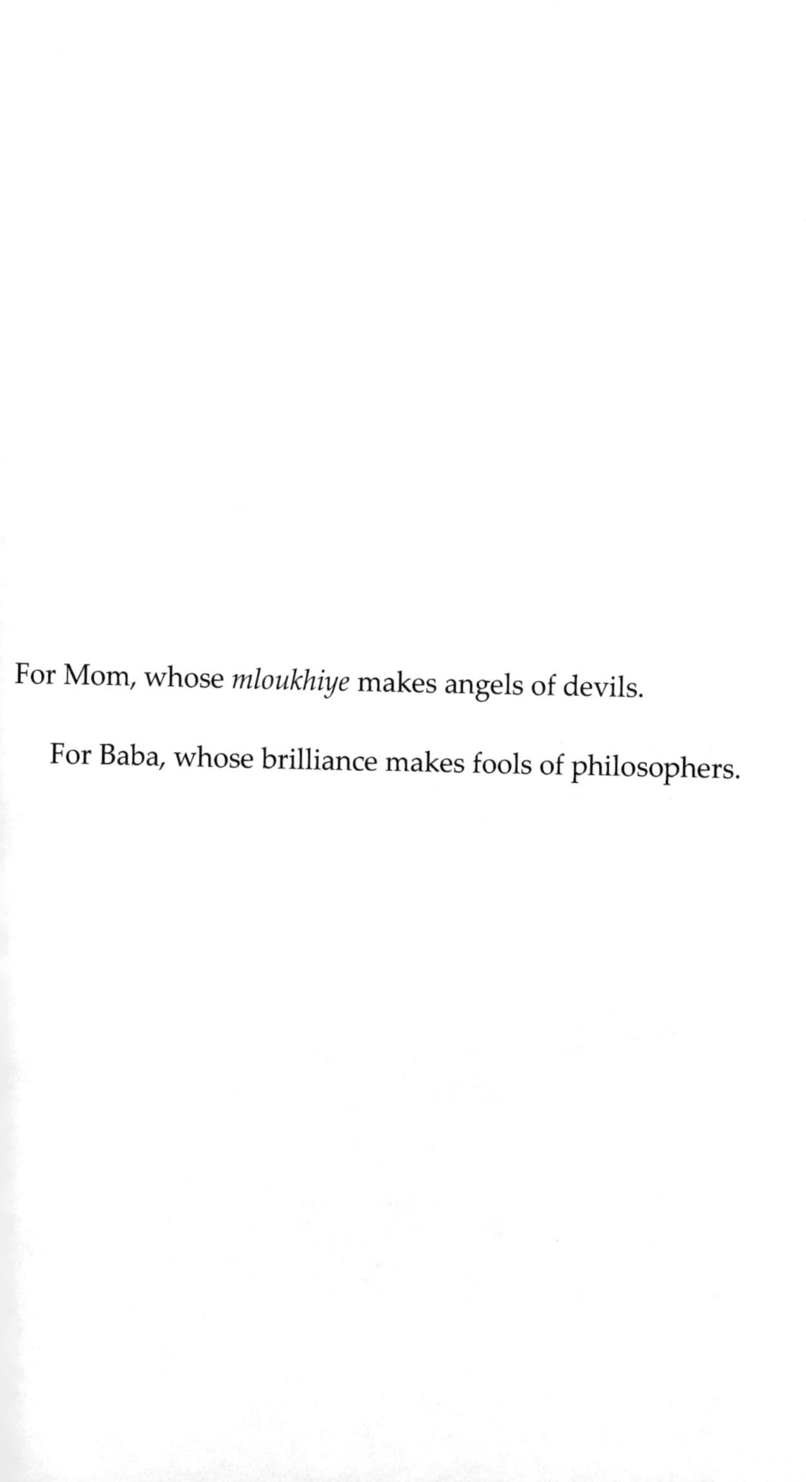

For Mom, whose *mloukhiye* makes angels of devils.

For Baba, whose brilliance makes fools of philosophers.

CONTENTS

ACKNOWLEDGMENTS

The number of people who helped this book come into fruition are countless, for every piece of it evokes echoes of individuals I know and have known. Even so, there are a handful of people who laid their hands upon my work prior to its publication. Those are the ones who I would like to thank here.

John Mungiello, for your gorgeous cover art, without which this book would be fruitless.

Alex Azar, for lending me a writer's eye.

Natalia, for your careful hand.

Rick, for your scrupulous analyses.

Mike, for your steadfast reassurance.

Dan Keyser, for facilitating the first word of this collection.

Dr. Travis Timmerman, for your invaluable insights about "Rory at the Falls."

Joey, for being a Joey.

And Jazz, for being a good helper.

PROLOGUE

The angels hid the stars beneath their wings
Until the world's golden light melted away.
Amongst the remnants of the stars
There remained a traveler.

He rested his head on an asteroid
Barreling towards a blue planet.
He felt not the cold of this new galaxy
For he was enveloped in dream.

Eventually the traveler awoke in dirt
And found beside him a journal.
Inside it were words written in ink.
He did not recognize the hand.

WAR

HOLLOWED GROUND

Our fathers
Who art no longer
Hollowed be their names.

For the trenches bloat with blood like Venetian canals run red.
Generations of skull and sinew plaster the twisted tunnels.
The dirt shudders at the familial flesh.

The land is foul and fruitless.
The crops have not seen rotation.
There is nothing to eat but dust.

It is evidently betrayal to follow in the footsteps of the first father.
One need only open his eyes to witness the calamity.
This is what happens when man succumbs to the succubus that is his grandfather's bloodlust.

CARMENGROVE AT MIDNIGHT

The scent of burning roses fills the air.
Sweetness aflame.
Innocence stolen.
Honey spoiled.
Every moment death.

Flaming flowers fall from grace.
Wilting petals wither to ash.
Thornéd stems are a futile protection.
Beauty is defenseless against the cut of the sword.
The scent of burning roses reeks like rape.

Burning roses fall upon Carmengrove at midnight
And the Devil is still asleep.

KEYSER'S DANCE

I.
A man with a decorated chest coughs.
Those around the table bow to him
Like war horses acquiescing to their rider.

II.
The forest hides its face
Ashamed.

III.
Lucifer looks up from his sweltering throne.
At last, his wife has delivered him twins!

IV.
A young girl watches in wonder
As a magnificent cloud of cotton candy rises from the
    ground
And eats her.

V.
The Sun longs for the Earth
But a black veil prevents him from touching her.
Who will warm the bones of the pitiable planet?

VI.
Diplomacy rolls in its grave.
Its tattoos fade to nothing.

VII.

Young men are pulled from work
To be put to work
To earn a wage
To wage war.

VIII.

A clownfish searches for his son
Or any other sign of life.

IX.

Orchestrators of this tuneless symphony sip white wine on a remote shore
In celebration of their triumphant piece.

X.

He watches and wonders why His Son's blood was not enough.

THE FORGE

Some time ago, I was afflicted with a question that demanded more than one mind, and so I invited Jacob and Esau to supper. Having a cunning humor about me, I prepared lentil stew for the three of us. Though I am sure the stew perturbed Esau and embarrassed Jacob, the brothers indulged me and ate well. When they finished eating, I raised my question. I asked, "Should man keep a forge?"

Esau used his dining cloth to wipe his bearded mouth and said to me, "Every beast is a soldier. Wolves of the woodland use their noses to discern blood from the fragrances of the pines. Eagles use God's eyes to spy from the clouds. Snakes carry pots of poison in their bellies to sicken and scourge their enemies. Even the butterfly bears a weapon nuanced and tactical, for written in her colored wings is deception.

"But man is a beast without claws. His eyes are weak, for he cannot see afar. His ears are unreliable, for he hears only what he would like. When he runs or swims, he tires quickly. Naked, a man bears no arms. This is why he takes up the blacksmith's hammer and forges himself claws of steel."

In turn, Jacob responded, "You are right to say that man bears no claws. This should be proof enough that he was never meant to enter the fray with beasts. Killing to settle scores is the way of animals, but man has mind to achieve the same end. Let man abandon his forge and sharpen instead the light of his mind."

"No, that is not the way," Esau said. "To seize a man's forge is to revoke his ability to fight in a world bereft with violence, a world he inherits by birthright. However one man might detest his father and mother for bringing him into a world of war, he still inherits his birthright. Let man have his forge."

Jacob seemed ready to respond, but I raised an interjecting hand and said, "I would like to think Jacob correct, but some men are like animals. I say, let man have his forge."

LECTURE HALL

Is it not a shame when the academic dies
    Waiting for his students to fill the lecture hall?
That is to say, is it not a shame when the academic asks,
    "When will you learn?"
And is met with no response?

REIKO'S DOLL

Reiko peered across the ruins. Wrinkles fringed her eyes, wrinkles branded by age and imbued by the sun. Hardly a thing was left standing. Every shop had been ground to dust. Every tree had been slain or set aflame. There was nothing to scavenge from the community's carcass, nothing to salvage save for Reiko's doll.

With the strength of a woman who had lost, she overturned concrete slabs and climbed hills of rubble. No crack or crevasse went unsearched. Reiko breathed dust and death as she labored. Her old bones ached, but the ache was a trifle when put up against the desperate longing buried in her bosom. Ignorant of the cuts on her hands, she dug and heaved.

Quickly, it seemed, darkness fell upon the ruins. When the sweat on her forehead grew cold, Reiko stopped searching and fell to her knees. She looked to the moon and pleaded to the God she feared had forgotten her. When she heard nothing but the heavy thumping of her heart, she put her eyes to the ground and at last found her granddaughter's remains.

ON CRUELTY

The notion of cruelty is a dangerous trap.
For when one deems an excess of violence to be intolerable
This implies a measure of violence that is tolerable.

Consider how drunkenness is said to be a vice
Where one or two drinks is no vice at all.
Such is the skeleton of cruelty.

One blow may be justified, but not a flurry.
A palm, perhaps, but not a fist.
To the chest, but not the face.

Oh, but the distance between violence and cruelty
Is less than a fraction of a hair!
Only a fool sees chasm where there is convergence.

BLOOD ORANGES

Let us eat blood oranges
Fruits sweet with the taste of citrus ignorance.

We shall wear black
For we are in mourning for ourselves.

It is a strange procession.
Have you ever seen the dead mourn the gravedigger?

PEACE

WATERMELON SEEDS

A week after the wedding, my father and I were basking on the side of a green hill. The sky was calm and blue, undisturbed by even a cloud. Gusts of warm wind rustled the grass. It was he and I and the clement sun. I sat and listened to the sound of my father cracking *bizir* with his teeth. Watermelon seeds were his favorite snack in the summertime. The stillness was only disturbed when Baba reached into his pocket and took out a chrome lighter. I couldn't hide the surprise from my face. My father smoked *argileh,* but never cigarettes. I wondered why he had a lighter.

Baba remained fixated on the sky. Staring into the blue, he said, "It's easy to cause problems. It's easy to be destructive, to ruin your relationships, to give people reasons to hate you. It's easy to be vile, to be crude. Very easy."

He turned his face to the lighter, and with one roll of the finger, it sprouted orange flame. The flame floated above Baba's thumb and held steady against the breeze. He said, "When you harbor anger, pain, hate, those feelings don't rest. They move, they have energy. They burn and burn until they consume your mind and your being. But you have a choice. You can use the fire to scathe, or you can use it to warm."

Baba eased the flame onto a patch of grass that lay between the both of us. The grass caught fire and melted to shrewd black crisps. The menacing flame continued to roll across the ground and eat the neighboring blades. Baba said, "When you start a fire in any odd place, it spreads. It's relentless. It moves in unpredictable ways. But if you gather a stack of wood and light a fire in the hearth, the fire will serve you well."

When I peeled my eyes from the burning earth, Baba was holding the lighter out to me. "Take it," he said.

I obeyed and weighed the device in my hands, contemplating what I would use it for. Sometimes Faris and I would borrow Baba's reading glasses and use them to burn ants. Maybe we could use the lighter instead. Baba stamped out the flame with his foot and took another handful of *bizir*.

LONGEVITY MOUNTAIN

Sky rises.

Labor bends the bones.
Muscles roast with fire.
Hands throb deep purple.
Limbs dilute to water.

Sky reaches.

Heat afflicts the head with levity.
Eyes look upon the work with disgust.
Knees tremble at the body's demands.
Strain plucks the spine like a harp.

Sky falls.

Tongue tastes bread and wine.
Back feels water run down.
Passion finds a companion.
Sleep.

DEAD MAN,

Tell me. Do you know the trick? Do you know how to reap victory from the grave? The philosophers and mystics purported to know, but they fell short of the mark. Contrary to their claims, the answer is not a legacy or a good life. The dead choose not their legacies just as the living dictate not the gossip spoken away from their ears. Likewise, a good life is a good life only. After death, what is life but a dream?

So I ask you again. Do you know the trick? Do you know how to reap victory from the grave? Do you know how to reach your hands through grave soil and grab the throats of those who wished harm unto you when you walked?

Dead man, listen. All you must do is proffer a gift to your enemy. This gift is not to be of gold or silk, but of flesh. To reap victory from the grave, you must proffer your cheek to your enemy. For if you turn your cheek to your enemy, your enemy will certainly kill you. He will raise his club and bash your head without mercy until your brain stains the ground and your blood runs for miles. Your soul will be swallowed by the dirt, and you will rot. Remember, this is but a sacrifice, for you will wring his neck in due time.

Dead man, think. Emboldened by his false strength, your enemy will approach the next man with a raised club expecting deference. However, the man your enemy approaches, knowing not the trick I have shared with you, will fight, and your enemy, filled with hubris, will be unprepared to take blows, and will be overcome. He will die stupefied. This is a true victory.

Yes, you will have died in pursuit of this triumph, but your living hands will be free of blood. The things that happen after you die will not incriminate you once you are entombed, for the dead belong to the worms, and the worms do not judge.

SOLACE

On cool summer nights
The sun is a tangerine
The moon peels away

THE MAILMAN

The mailman comes in the morning bearing packages labelled with my name and address alone. When I received the first anonymous package, I was curious. After all, who would send *me* something unprompted? My curiosity morphed to dismay, however, when I discovered that the packages entombed black spirits.

Ghoulish, ghastly things they were. Cold and ungiving, they were not gifts, but vexes. What witch did I know who would dare bring such calamities to my doorstep? I knew not a person who dealt in dark spirits.

Perplexed by the question of the culprit, I eventually suspected the mailman to be the devious orchestrator. He was, after all, a stranger. I knew nothing of him but his face and his occupation. But the suspicion did not survive long, for the mailman hadn't any feasible grievance with me, nor I with he.

Aimless obsession tore through my mind like a tumbling weed. To sate the yearning, I decided to inquire as to the origin of the cursed packages. One morning, when the mailman came to my doorstep, I asked him, "Who is sending me all of these packages?" But the mailman responded only by laying a package down at my feet.

When the mailman disappeared from my sight, I collected the bundle and brought it into the house. Dreading the familiar black that came with every unaddressed package, I unwrapped the parcel. Inside was a letter. Its words were written in my hand.

JENIN

Are you
Are you
Coming to Jenin?

THE STARS IN PARADISE

They say that when an angel plants a seed, it grows into Paradise.
I happen to know a person whose eyes harbor constellations.
She must have swallowed a seed while eating blessed fruit.

I walk through gardens adorned with greenery.
The fragrant orchards bear fruit sweeter than the music in the wind.
Little miracles, the flowers are in full bloom, and their petals are bursting with color.

I hear a honeyed harmony rolling across the vineyards.
The wind carries a voice that reaffirms my heart's foundations.
I have seen the crooked bend straight in the breeze of endless spring.

I tell you, my world is illuminated by the light in her eyes.
Who could sleep when the stars in Paradise shine more brightly than the sun?
Not I.

EVERLASTING LIFE

With every exhale, you affirm that life is borrowed.
If this makes you afraid, I can only implore you to breathe deeply.

Someday you will die, but you will not find yourself alone.
You will be reunited with friends departed.

What is more, the friends who shed a tear at your grave will join you when their time comes.
After is not lonely like it is so often now.

God is your Father, and he bids that his children be under one roof.
This is peace.

RESPECT

RORY AT THE FALLS

The roaring falls tossed torrents of water down, down, down to the black far below. Rory doffed his shoes and planted his bare feet on the wet rock overhanging the falls. He stood encapsulated by the sound of the water's goading. One step forward, and he would plummet a long way down until his body broke on the basin. Rory knew this, for he had come to the falls to die.

"Excuse me, lad! What are you doing up there?" Rory turned to find a man wearing fogged glasses staring up at him from behind the rock. Rory thought him a wanderer.

"I'm just watching," Rory said.

"Watching from all the way up there, with your shoes off? It's dangerous, boy. One misstep and that'll be the end of you. You'll crack like a dropped egg."

With as much patience as he could muster, Rory asked, "Are you lost, sir?"

The man with fogged glasses scratched his head. "Lost? No, boy. I'm just passing through, on my way home. You should come down from there."

Realizing that the man had stopped solely to pester him, Rory allowed his patience to flutter away. "I'm trying to enjoy the view in peace. Be on your way. Night will soon fall."

The man with the fogged glasses folded his arms. "You're not here for the view. There are plenty of places around the falls that give a better look at less the risk. Do you want to die, boy? Because it seems that way."

Rory considered refuting the man until he realized he hadn't any need to justify himself. Soon as he had his privacy, he would leap, and he would die. Rory stood silent.

The man with fogged glasses put thinking fingers to his chin. "Fine, you want to die. What of me, then?"

Rory looked down at the man with frustration. "What of you? You have no stake here. Be on your way."

"Oh, I have no stake?"

"Of course you have no stake! What obligation do you have to me? Go without guilt. It's foolish to assume a burden that doesn't fall upon your shoulders."

The man with fogged glasses grunted. "Guilt is no concern of mine. I didn't put you up on that rock. Think a moment, and tell me. What right have you to take your own life?"

"I have every right," Rory responded.

The man with fogged glasses raised a brow. "And what of another's life? Do you have the right to take another's life?"

"Not another's, but my own."

"But you're flesh and blood like any other person. If you don't have the right to take a person's life, how could you justify throwing yourself down into the water?"

"Because my life is my own," Rory growled.

"Your life must be worth less than all the others, then."

Rory shook his head. "It doesn't matter what it's worth. What matters is I'm done with it. If somebody sets my crop alight, he's a pillager, but if I set my own crop alight, I'm a fool, but I have a right to be. So call me a fool and move on."

The man with fogged glasses answered, "You know life isn't to be taken because you say you wouldn't take another's, yet you'll take your own. If you don't think your life matters less than another's, then you must think everyone else's life matters as little as yours. In that case, I might as well jump."

"Who are you to talk like this? You see nothing. Your glasses are fogged," Rory said.

The man with fogged glasses bowed, acquiescing the point. "They're fogged because I've come to the edge of the falls, and the waters' mist has clouded my lenses. I've been standing here for hours trying to muster the courage to leap, and every syllogism has brought me closer to leaping. Thank you for your help, lad."

The man with the fogged glasses charged towards the roaring falls and threw himself into the black. He fell down, down, down until his body broke on the water. Along with the splash came an echo. *"Philosophy is poor remedy for an ailing heart."*

MARBLE MEN

When a man is living
His life is painted
In hues of gray and gold.

And then he dies
And his life becomes
A saccharine mirage.

Monuments are monuments
Not to men who once stood
But to memories misremembered.

Many think marble a mirror
But stone cannot reflect
The spirit of those departed.

Even a sculptor most adept with mallet and chisel
Cannot impress a man's wisdom
Into a marble furrow.

We may think marble weighs more than flesh
But the soul sits heavy
Between the ribs.

Once the soul leaves the body
One cannot capture it ever again
Not even by means of marble.

SUNFLOOD

You encroached upon me
And sought strife with my kin
But never did I wish
Death upon you.

I spent a dewy morning
In the memorial field
And watched your House's banner
Sway from the ramparts.

That morning
I bathed in the coldest sunflood
For the field was bright
But the air held no mirth.

I cannot ask for your friendship
Nor can we make amends
But you can be certain
I will pay my respects.

FORTY MANGOES

A monkey brought mangoes to town
And suddenly he was king.

MOM AND DAD

Mom and Dad
Composed my life
In Arabic script.

Mom and Dad
Fed me milk and dates
So I would never starve.

Mom and Dad
Brought me to church
To introduce me to *Suryoyo*.

Mom and Dad
Gave me sisters
To teach me patience.

Mom and Dad
Showed me goodness
That I might turn from vice.

Now I walk
To reap reward
For dearest Mom and Dad.

NEKO LOST

On the night of the Samurai's Banquet, a thief conducted a heist in the heavens. Typically, any living man who dared to intrude upon the samurai's heavenly quarters would find himself sliced in two, but this night was different. While the samurai were most always diligent, their heavenly homes most always impenetrable, the night of the Samurai's Banquet was one of indulgence. With food and wine aplenty, the samurai ate heartily and drank in excess. After the feast, the samurai congregated in the gardens. They stayed up well into the night recounting tales of their victories and, as the wine settled, sharing their most bitter regrets. These festivities presented the thief with an opportunity to infiltrate the heavens that he might take what he had long desired.

The thief climbed a ladder through the atmosphere and into the heavens until he stumbled into a grand abode belonging to Samurai Gohan, the scholar-samurai as famous for his penmanship as for his swordsmanship. The thief had before him all of the samurai's riches, gems and jewels and ornaments and artifacts that gleamed of their own accord. Scrolls of ancient wisdom lined bookshelves carved from black oak. But the thief hadn't come for the riches or the wisdom.

Resting on the warrior's bed was his companion dog, Neko. People of every province caught glimpses of Neko when the sun was high and the weather was warm, for it was in such weather that Samurai Gohan would walk Neko through the clouds. The thief had no doubt that Neko was the most valuable possession amongst all of the riches in the samurai's abode, for its beauty was unmatched by any earthly creature. And so he snatched the dog and retreated to the earth, certain he could sell Neko for a significant sum.

Upon returning to his quarters the following morning, Samurai Gohan immediately noticed that his precious companion dog was missing. By the very smell of the room, the samurai knew that his quarters had been invaded by a mortal. Enraged, he threw himself down to the earth to seek the thief who had seized his beloved dog. He pored over every principality in every province in search of Neko. In his pursuit, he crushed boulders underfoot like eggs, split trees with his hands like chopsticks, and ignited caves with the fire of his ire as he inspected every crevasse of every hill and plain, to no avail.

When the samurai's search proved unfruitful, he drew his blade and looked towards the highest mountain in the land with a killing gaze. Driven to wrath by his misfortune, the samurai swung his blade through the mountain's peak, dismembering it from its earthen body. The mountain belched black rock and stained the sky with darkness. The angry geyser threw ropes of flame every which way. Liquid fire, glowing hot like a smith's furnace, rolled down the mountain's tremorous slopes. The burning river charged towards the villagers who made their homes around the mountain, and the people ran, but they could not outrun the samurai who sought his companion dog, Neko.

As Samurai Gohan watched fire chase the earth away, he heard a bark from below. With the force of a thunderclap, Samurai Gohan charged down the mountain, sword drawn, ready to cut down those who had stolen his beloved Neko. As it happened, the samurai reached the foot of the mountain in time to witness liquid flame swallow his dog, who had tried in earnest to outrun the calamity, but could not.

That is why the once-tranquil mountain is volatile today. It often rumbles and quakes with Samurai Gohan's anger. This should serve as a lesson to all. If you are to show any respect, show it to the heavens, lest fire make ash of your home.

CHERRY BLOSSOM

The most miserable man who ever lived
        Demanded more of a cherry blossom.

SHAJARA (TREE)

I have three grandfathers.
    Two are George.
    One is Gibran.
I have six uncles.
    Issa.
    Ibrahim.
    Jule.
    Suhale.
    George.
    And Darwish.
I have too many cousins to name.
    Amongst them are Rumi and Qabbani.

My kind have cultivated words in a place where nothing grows but enmity.
We are a *shajara* whose roots drink water where there is no water to be found.
Watch me erect a library more impressive than the one buried under Baghdad.
Watch me weave tapestries of verse more splendid than those of the Bedouins.

I am the grandson
    The nephew
        The cousin
            The heir.

You will soon pluck fruit from my branch.

CULTURE

TEA

Everywhere they go they ask for tea.
They drink with lemon and honey when they are sick of feeling alone.
One moment without a steaming cup in hand is torturous.

Everywhere they go they ask for tea.
Black with sugar like everyone else.
Like parrots talking to parrots, they mimic each other and sip.

Everywhere they go they ask for tea.
They drink with mint and milk to taste sophistication.
All they know is talk of the brew.

Everywhere they go they ask for tea.
The scent of hibiscus tempts them to swallow.
They reach for a cup without first contemplating whether or not they are thirsty.

Everywhere they go they ask for tea.
They drink chamomile to soothe their swaying stomachs.
It is as if they are made nauseous by the fact of their habit.

THUMBS

After spending so much time twiddling our thumbs
It is no wonder we've found favor in our fingers.

Our thumbs, once proof of humanity's supremacy, have
    fallen to folly.
It is sad to remember that our thumbs once belonged to the
    craftsmen
For today they belong only to gluttons who eat with both
    hands.

LAY ME DOWN

Lay me down just for a night.
Your face will fade to silhouette.
Your name will burn away with the passion
Until even the thought of you disappears.

You are a phoenix.
You are creature with such potential.
Yet I place my bootheel on your cheek
And condemn you.

You know what I am.
You are naive for succumbing to my tricks.
You are like a baby who has stumbled upon the gut of Hell
In search of the breast of the Earth.

Lay me down just for a night.
The darkness will conceal my tears.
Your ignorance of your own worth
Aggrieves me.

BABEL

A city without a heart is
A carcass of empty delights
A ferris wheel unmoving
A river of still water.

PURPLE POTIONS

An impatient congregation forms a line outside the Alchemist's workshop. Inside, the Alchemist's apprentices bustle about to concoct elixir after elixir. The public is thirsty for purple potions, and the Alchemist expects his apprentices to deliver.

The apprentices flow around one another intuitively, not even grazing shoulders as they pass one another. Their purple robes sweep about them as they step hither and thither around their work benches. They work with the vigor of bulls and the swiftness of hummingbirds, well-trained in their craft, well-disciplined in the art of alchemy.

Without pausing even to wipe the sweat from their faces, they charge forward, handling beakers and chemicals. They measure and pour, shake and scald. The purple potion is no inconsequential concoction, after all. Precision is essential.

One by one, the people of the congregation step up to the benches to receive their potions, those which they hallow like communion wine, and drink them down. The purple potion spills through their veins, giving them enough courage to face the day.

Seeing all this, the Alchemist is pleased, for the purple potions distract the world of his work, which he enjoys conducting quietly.

THE BARDS

I see nothing wrong with looking to the past for present
guidance
But the musings of dead men should not inform eternity.

In my estimation
Socrates and the rest are bards at best.

We ought to enjoy them, but to submit?
Not to the bards.

PAY ME

I will bury you, so long as you pay me.
I will even murder you and deliver the news to your family, if the price is right.
I will sicken you with false medicine, so long as you compensate me.
I will write your eulogy and deliver it, if the price is fair.

I will send you flowers, so long as they are on sale.
I will attend your funeral, so long as I already own a suit that fits.
I will send my condolences via check, so long as my bank account can endure the strain of your passing.
I will tell my children of your life, so long as your heart was generous.

For my favor is purchased with commodity.
My soul is curried in currency.
My virtue is contingent on value.
My happiness is economic.

Pay me, I implore you.
I will gladly sell my gratitude.
I will be loyal to the end.
So long as you pay me.

THE STATE OF THINGS

There is a sun burning brightly
Under the ocean
And there is a moon casting daylight
In the afternoon.

There is a mountain hanging upside down
From the sky
And there is rain falling inside the room
Horizontally.

There are planets
In my spoon
And there is a sesame seed in the sky
The size of Jupiter.

This is the state of things.

CELEBRATION

THE BAR

On the first night of winter, two men found themselves sitting at a Bar tended by the Fates. There was a man named Hebi who was sipping his second whiskey, and there was a man named Tenshi who had yet to touch his mug of ale. Hebi was not one to see drink wasted, and so he turned to the other man and asked, "Is there something wrong with your drink?"

Tenshi looked down into the murky ale and said, "Most nights I have a taste for ale, but tonight I am thinking there is no better drink than sunshine."

Hebi put his glass to his lips and said, "Sunshine may be the most wholesome drink, but man prefers to sip from a more vulgar cup."

Tenshi shrugged and slumped into himself. "Man's preference for the vulgar cup is folly. Where the vulgar cup sets a man's insides aflame for only a short while, sunshine is an imperishable hearth that nourishes the body. Surely you cannot say that the vulgar cup is preferable."

Hebi struck his glass against the Bar and said, "The vulgar cup may affect a man for only a time, but at least it serves as a companion to those who are awake when the sun has fallen to its cradle beneath the horizon. The sun is a lazy friend."

"Aye," Tenshi began. "You are right to say that the sunshine subsides, but it subsides for only a short while. God always brings respite at the dawn. By contrast, the vulgar cup is a pitiful vessel that offers no respite. It muddles man's sights so that he stumbles about aimlessly, without direction, until his belly can churn the poison out. Consider how sunshine lights the day so that one may see where he may walk. Surely you cannot say that the vulgar cup offers such clarity."

"Ah, but you cannot say that sunshine offers any more clarity than the vulgar cup," Hebi responded. "You see, sunshine is an oppressive thing. It reveals everything, taunting man, because man cannot possibly see all of the world's wonders in his short life. The sunshine may serve as a North Star for those who are prone to losing themselves in the world, but for those who know the truth of life, the vulgar cup is preferable, for it shows man the true character of his spirit."

Tenshi was perplexed by Hebi's words. "The vulgar cup does not draw from the wellspring of man's spirit, it sifts Cain's soil, which is bereft with toxicity. God's greatest wellspring is sunshine, a fountain forged above Eden and bountiful for all."

Hebi raised a brow at that. "I know your God. Is your God not of the vulgar cup?"

Faced with a question he could not bring himself to answer, Tenshi looked down at the mug of ale before him and scowled. "You are no friend to me. You are proof that the vulgar cup is for the serpents, for you talk with a forked tongue. Who would like to converse with a cunning man? Not I." Tenshi took the mug of ale into his hands and drank it down. Surely the sun would shine in the morning.

ALIBI

Some days are hard-fought
While others are gentle.
The median is a turbulent sea
Alive and unremitting.

There is no end or edge to the ocean
So we sail across the seas
Hoping to find friends
Amongst the fish.

I recall a time when I traversed the ocean without a companion with whom I could break bread.
I did not regret trading one horizon for the next
For I lived unremarkably.
I kept my own company and buried my heart.

I had long believed that being at peace with oneself was paramount
But I have since learned that people are not meant to dine alone.
We are to eat with our friends and sleep with our lovers.
Time alone is for academics and the displeased.

While I lament that I did not lament my travels
When those around me cried and rejoiced for the water behind them
I feel the water beneath my ship today
And breathe deeply.

CHAPSTICK

The old are mixed with the young
Yet the old seem to be dancing on an island of their own.

The spectators admire the proficiency of their elders
And dream of enduring love, seeing their own faces in the aged.

It is pure fantasy for those who cannot dance
But perhaps it is not always to be fantasy.

Perhaps as one ages, one shrugs the notion of "can't"
And steps to the floor to shake his bones of their dust.

YESTERDAY'S THUNDER

When one remembers that the day is coming
Thunder rolls.
When one remembers that the day is coming
Thunder rolls.

One is not compelled to whisper that the day is near
But to cry out from the mountain's top.
The shout strikes keen ears
And those who hear gather in the square to join hands.

This happens from day to day amongst the people.
When the time finally comes, the crowd sings and sways.
Sometimes they break things
But they congregate to stand and listen first and foremost.

At home there is whiskey
But here the mind ascends to heaven.
Even those who enjoy the amber brew are taken to the skies
To live a night secluded from the planet.

When the morrow arrives, the Thunder will have vanished
But from time to time
The people will hear echoes of yesterday's Thunder
And smile.

SOMETHING SHORT

The heart can only hold so much.

It is certainly a sad thing when it is emptied
But it will eventually come to hold new things.

This is cause for celebration, however sad.

ON THRILL

Man straps himself into a metal contraption from which he cannot escape. He submits to the Leviathan that he may be throttled upside down and tossed every which way by the roaring beast.

Man sees that he does not have wings beneath his arms, yet he leaps from the mountains even still. He cuts through the air by his determination alone.

Man sips venom delivered by the vulgar cup even though it blackens his innards. He kisses the chalice even on Sunday.

Man forages not to fortify his bones and muscles, but to satisfy his tongue. His tongue is tied up with his impulsive mind, which seeks pleasure above all else, and this union results in the neglect of his body.

In light of these truths, one might think man a most pitiable creature. Aye, there is no doubt that man hunts for treacherous thrills in perpetuum, but perhaps his desire for thrill is not base. Perhaps his ready submission to thrill speaks to his spirit.

Perhaps we chase thrill that we may brush shoulders with death, if only for fleeting moments. Perhaps bearing the badge of one who has come away from death unscathed emboldens man and elevates him, in his mind, to a level at which only God stands.

Aye, man will die, but so long as he can deceive himself, he will. For the weight of man's mortality presses heavy upon his soul, and if illusion offers respite, illusion man will choose.

SEVENTEEN SHIRLEY TEMPLES

Me and my friends form
A ring around a rose.
All eyes are on the bride
So we are free for the night.

Everyone else is tall
But the forest of legs is navigable.
We cut through
Seeking Versailles.

We find the chamber
Flooded with marble and light.
Some get lost amongst the columns.
We run up and down the stairs.

Me and my friends
We come to find the bar.
All the men are sweating over it.
Nobody pays us any mind.

We look over the counter
To see what wonders await.
Two barkeeps serve glasses to all.
We try our luck.

Even then I knew excess
Tied in cherry stems.
Cheers to my cousin.
Seventeen Shirley Temples.

MY FALCON,

When you find yourself mourning, finish quickly
For life is to be a celebration.

Cry if you must, but know that your tears fall into a
reservoir
Where they are indiscernible from all the others.

The shine of wonder in your eyes
That is yours alone.

Let your life be a constellation of stars
As opposed to an ocean of sorrows.

STRUGGLE

FIRE BESIDE THE BEDSIDE

In my dreams I heard a sound like Satan licking his lips. My nightmare actualized when I opened my eyes to witness the fire's sinister crackling. Flame was climbing the walls of my room and reaching for the ceiling that I may be confined in a hellish cage. The heat of the inferno raging beside my bedside was of a magnitude I had never thought I would ever experience.

The Devil spoke in smoke, and his whispers rose from the floor. Black clouds obscured the room in an apocalyptic haze. I knew that my life was to end. The only uncertain thing was whether I would sooner suffocate by the ash in the air or burn like a candlewick. All I could do was lay there, immobile, watching the world end from my bed.

When musing upon death, some proclaim that they would like to pass away in bed—in their sleep, particularly—trusting this to be a peaceful way to depart from the earth. When one pays that notion thought, it seems sensible. After all, a sudden affliction like a fall or a heart attack is a parcel delivered by chaos. Conversely, the bed is a place of stability. One goes to bed to rest. Why, then, should the bed not be the stage for one's final sleep?

Ah, but this neat notion held no water when I awoke to the fire beside my bedside. There I lay upon this shrine of peace, yet I saw nothing but fire and felt nothing but fear. I had always thought I would fall into a sort of wizened complacency in those final moments. I wouldn't think too much about what was to come, only about what I had reaped during the time I was able-bodied. I would see my life painted in visions of euphoric haze. I would be surrounded by my loved ones—those who had lived as long as I—and drift away into sleep with gladness in my heart and the look of a stoic warrior on my face. But there I was, overcome by primal fear, feeling every ache in my aged bones, surrounded by nobody, dying in dream.

COME TO THE HOLY CITY!

Come to the Holy City!

A place of false pretense.
A place of fictitious narratives.
A place of kings and Martin Luther Kings.
A complicated place.

Come to the Holy City!

A place of incomplete thoughts and unpunctuated sentences.
A place of half-truths and quarter-pounders.
A place of jokes without punchlines and problems without solutions.
A place of strife above all else.

Come to the Holy City!

OUR OWN SYMPOSIUM

We worship *ad hominem,* yet our devotion is misguided. How are we to understand ourselves if we do not drink with our enemies?

WRESTLING AT PENUEL

You have thrust me into a world that seeks to consume me
    Yet I prostrate myself at your feet.
You have sheltered my loved ones away from me
    Yet I submit myself to you.
You have filled my mind with questions that confound me
    Yet I do not speak ill of you.
You have contrived a sphere of such madness
    Yet I surrender to you.

I have seen good people face horrific tragedies
    Yet I do not curse you.
I have sinned through all my senses, and I despise this
    Yet I do not denounce you.
I have denied myself fruit for bread
    Yet I do not turn away from you.
I have stumbled on the path you have paved for me
    Yet I walk it nonetheless.

My compassion is not infinite
    Yet I come to you, for there seems to be no greater
        teacher in forgiveness.

SHADOWBOXING

One night while making his rounds, Jaar heard a faint noise coming from Prince Gethryn's chambers. Careful not to make a sound, Jaar put his ear to the door. If the boy was in any danger, Jaar was prepared to cut down the threat with the sword he wore on his waist, but there was no danger in the palace tonight. Much to Jaar's displeasure, the prince was whimpering.

Jaar growled to himself. Whimpering wouldn't do. Gethryn had far too many responsibilities to be blubbering in the night. Postured to harangue the boy, Jaar threw the door open, and the silhouetted prince shot up in his bed. Jaar didn't care that he had scared him. "It's Jaar. Talk to me, boy. What ails you?"

Flustered, Gethryn said, "Nothing, sir. I'm fine."

Jaar leaned on the prince's bedpost. "I heard you crying. There's no sense in lying. Talk to me so we can handle this without your father. What ails you, boy?"

After a sigh, Gethryn confessed, "A woman, sir."

Jaar's expression became stony, though it was concealed by the darkness. "Oh? How does one catch such an ailment? Leaving the house without a coat? Eating an undercooked slice of ham?"

"She's no germ, sir," Gethryn explained. "But my stomach is twisted and I don't know how to untwist it. She's a fat mystery, and I haven't a clue what to do about it."

Jaar instinctively stroked the pommel of his sword. "Well lad, using 'fat' anywhere near talk of her is foolish enough for three men. So I assume you're accustomed to flubbing up, with a tongue unguarded as that. What've you done to anger her?"

Gethryn's silhouette shrugged. "I haven't done any wrong, I've just...done. And she's unhappy."

"Well, what is it you're doing? You must be doing something, otherwise she hates you for breathing."

Gethryn let his head fall into his hands. "Sometimes it seems like she *does* hate me for breathing."

Jaar clenched his sword's hilt. "Lad, there's nothing stronger in this world than a woman's fury. If she hated you, you'd be dead on the floor. Listen closely, boy. There's a notion many your age seem to have. You all seem to think you're gods, invincible and able to conquer the skies. Be that as it may, you will never have the might to nudge a woman even an inch in the direction you want her to go."

"But—"

"Let me finish. You're concerned that she's upset. That's fine. But once you've tried your best to help her with her troubles, you have to step away. She has her own mind. Let her use it. If she's anyone worth your time, she'll come to you after she's finished her battle, apologize, and kiss you. Then you'll do it all over again. Understand?"

"...I think so," Gethryn responded.

"Right. Now go to sleep. If I catch you blubbering this late into the night again, I'll whip you so good you'll be blubbering into next year. And I'll whip you for blubbering then, too."

TEMPTATION

When sin perplexes you, remember:
Man does not indulge in forbidden fruit because he is hungry.

RAINWATER

I asked a priest, "Must a faithful man attend church to know God?"

He responded, "Can rainfall sate a man's thirst? Or is it better that he drinks from a wellspring?"

GIVE ME THE MOUNTAINS

You say I know nothing of struggle.
True, that I know nothing of yours.
But of mine, *you* know nothing.
Give me the mountains!

Tell me of your struggles, and I will give you my sympathies.
But my battles are for me and my circle alone, not for the wind.
I do not count myself a bird, but a boulder.
Give me the mountains!

What I have conquered in privacy you could not conquer in your dreams.
Sleep, and tell me of the beasts you face in your nightmares.
I have wrestled more fearsome beings awake.
Go count sheep, and give me the mountains!

Look, I hold all of the desert in my palm.
I collected the sand myself, plucking each grain from the ground with my own fingers.
Not a drop of water has touched my tongue in the whole pursuit.
And I am thirsty!

Hear me when I say I have swam seven seas.
Clueless, yes, but I have swam!

My father threw me into the deep when I was young, and
this is how I learned to persevere.
Give me the mountains!

I have found more questions than answers in the caves I
have dwelt armed only with a lantern dwindling dimly.
And it was not the daytime!
I have read, and I understand some.
Read me the definition of illiteracy, and give me the
mountains!

I have been stretched like hide between two posts and
beaten without mercy.
I lash out in anger.
Respite, a stone's throw away? No, a boulder's!
Give me the mountains!

For the world has sewn seeds upon my mind's connecting
threads.
And my heart has a hole shaped like God.
I may not be able to shoulder your burden, but I will
shoulder mine.
Give me the mountains!

WORDS

OATHBREAKER, BEWARE

Oathbreaker, beware!

If you break an oath you have made with me
You risk falling from my eyes.
For if I have made a bond with you
I have cast it in iron.

Our bond is not unbreakable
For I am not God
But to sever the chains
Is to spite me.

My life is finite
As is yours.
To waste our time
Is tragedy.

We are both marching towards the grave.
It is no small thing if we agree to keep company along this march for a certain time.
Thus, when you take a different path after pledging an oath to the contrary
You leave me closer to the grave with less company.

Shame on you
For breaking my trust.
God is witness
To your empty guarantees.

Oathbreaker, beware!

ET TU

Friends trade whispers in confidence, betraying others' confidence.
The broken silence of once-kept secrets disturbs the ground enough that it cracks.
The rustle of rumor shakes the trees until the leaves fall
Slowly.

Aye, enemies stab one another
But friends do so with smiles sweet enough that those betrayed doubt the knives in their guts.
What fool would look down at his impaled belly and question whether he had been stabbed?
Only a friend.

A THING OF WOODEN HANDIWORK

There are high words and low words.

The high are volleyed by the philosophers.
The low are thrown about in the bars.
Now some say that the language of the low
Ought not emerge from the mouths of the high-minded.

While I do find low words to be ugly and unpleasant
It must be said that the lowest dialect is not necessarily like
A tea bag steeping
In a mug of hot water.

Consider how a high speaker talks mazes before describing
a scoundrel as such
Where a low speaker can take one look at a man and mark
him a scoundrel.
A high speaker brandishes his encyclopedic vocabulary and
dizzies those who listen
Where the drunkest low speaker can make a clearer point
using half the words.

A high speaker sees a thing of wooden handiwork
With four legs and a high back
That is stained deep brown and polished to the shine
Where a low speaker sees a chair.

That is the difference between the high and the low.

NORTH FOREVER

Choose three letters and speak with them only.
Listen to yourself, and decide if you hear any sense.

Walk north forever and do not stop.
When you return to the place you began, tell me where
you've been.

Blue is a beautiful color, but it is not enough.
Would you ever know a sunset if but one color reigned?

I READ SPARINGLY

To read is to travel the world from end to end
For the world is written on papyrus.

That is what I believed when I was a boy
When my greatest friend was fiction.

Now I am older.
All I need to see the world is a passport.

This way is more expensive
And yet I read sparingly.

BIG SLICE

You can dress a piece of cake
In the finest frosting and fondant
But if she is not hungry
She will not eat.

BLACK COFFEE

The dawn is dark and lonely.
The room is cloaked in drear.
The air is dull and dismal.
He prefers to sit alone.

A branch breaks outside.
Rain raids the window.
He leans over his desk.
Tears roll from his eyes.

Black coffee sits unsipped.
Steam rises from the mug.
It turns and twists and fades away.
An elusive dance.

Outside is escape.
Sometimes he thinks to go.
In the end he keeps his seat
For he hasn't an umbrella.

SEPPUKU

Hand me a sword that I might slice open my belly
For it has come time for my *seppuku*, my fatal demise.

I, the poet, am confessing that words are nothing
Except sounds summoned by the fickle tongue.

Words are incapable of homicide
And yet I see them being regarded as killers.
I find this posture to be troubling
For I know that words cannot kill.

Words can rally men to do harm
And words can express the desire to inflict pain
But words themselves cannot strangle.
Words cannot destroy cities with atomic force.

Man can poeticize the power of words all he wants
But he cannot assert that language has the capacity to
plunge a knife into another man's heart.
For speech to bear any consequence
Others must hear it, and abide.

SILENCE

MY APOLOGY

My prisoner lay on the splintered floor. His clothes were stained, his white hair damp and tangled, his body slim and frail. Once a rabble rouser, now a fly in my palm, I sought to pluck answers from him, however hard he might resist. Knowing smart man's hemlock to be isolation, I had left him alone for some time. Surely now the man would break.

"Tell me what you know," I demanded.

To my dismay, the prisoner turned his silver eye to me and said, "I know nothing."

I had grown tired of the old man repeating himself. He had left me no choice but to adopt a more severe methodology. "Fine," I said. "You won't see a meal until you tell me what you know."

And so I left the prisoner alone in his wooden cell and made good on my word. I sent every chef and scullion out from the kitchens and forbid the man his food. Seeing bread and stew no longer, my prisoner suffered the gnashings of hunger. He writhed on the floor like a wounded dog. Even the most civilized of people turned wild when afflicted with the pangs of starvation. Surely now the man would transform into a beast and break at the thought of breaking bread.

So I came into the man's cell and demanded that he tell me what he knew.

Remarkably, the old man turned his silver eye to me and said, "I know nothing."

Evidently, I had failed to communicate to the man the lengths to which I was willing to go to extract an answer from him. I determined that I ought to instill fear upon the man to shatter his spirit.

I indicated to the guards that I wanted a basin of icy water brought into the prisoner's cell. They delivered it promptly. At my order, the guards contorted the frail prisoner until he was kneeling upright and seized his head and hair that he may remain so. Without support, the old man would have swayed one way or another and collapsed to the splintered ground.

I posed my request to him again. "Tell me what you know."

Again, the same response, in a voice faint as rustling leaves. "I know nothing."

"Unacceptable," I said.

At that, the guards plunged the prisoner's head into the frigid deep and held it there. The prisoner struggled. His sinewed hands grasped at nothing and his swollen feet kicked at the air. Desperate bubbles broke the top of the water in a hurried stream. Good. Soon he would give me what I wanted.

After a good bout of drowning, I motioned for the guards to relieve the prisoner. He came up from the water gasping. His wrinkled face was a sickly purple. His hair was soaked and heavy. The guards tossed him to the floor a sopping mess. Quaking where he lay, teeth chattering, the man looked broken. Now to see if he would crack.

"I ask you again. Tell me what you know."

Shivering, the prisoner shook his head. His tongue must have frozen. Ironic, as it was the man's tongue that had placed him at my feet. The temptation of knowledge is seductive, and the prisoner had flaunted his riches in the public. He was said to know more than any man. He was an agitator amongst the populace, certainly, but I would be a fool to neglect plucking his brain for my own enlightenment before I sent him to die.

"Guards, bring me the bamboo."

Whatever state the prisoner was in, his ears were working, for he sobbed into the floor at that. His tears were futile. A slice of me wanted to hang the prisoner by his entrails and leave him for the dogs without delay, but he purported to have knowledge of matters important to the spirit, and so I spared him his life in the interest of forcing his tongue.

The guards returned with a handful of bamboo shoots, each three inches long. They placed them in my palm and turned to the prisoner, picking him up from his defeated position and forcing him to his knees once again. His belabored breaths indicated that he objected, but I was more determined than he. The guards seized his right hand and offered it to me, a glorious gift.

The prisoner tried to clench his hand into a fist to protect his fingers, but my guards were stronger. His fingers were mine. I grasped the prisoner's forefinger and thrust the bamboo under his nail. He howled in pain, howled like the dog he was. It seemed that he had reached his limit, as had I. I posed the question to him again. "Tell me, you bastard. What do you know?"

"Nothing!" the prisoner howled. "I know nothing!"

Filled with ire, I grabbed the old man by his throat and put my forehead to his. I saw the fire in my eyes reflected in his silvers. I said, "Your reputation is that of a wise man. I know you wander the streets seeking to indoctrinate. You teach, so you must know. Do you think me a fool?"

The prisoner shook his head, frantic. Weeping, he pleaded, "Please, my finger!"

I released the prisoner's neck and drew the knife from my belt. Looking to address his plea, I severed his forefinger from his hand. I first thought myself a poet at that moment, for the finger I had severed was the finger he had used to point the youth towards knowledge many viewed as heretical. But I wanted to hear it. Furious, I shouted, "There, I've dealt with the finger! Now, speak! Tell me how you can claim to know nothing when the people speak of you being a sage who purports to know about earth and the heavens!"

Crying, Socrates lamented, "Those who say I know haven't listened to me at all. Don't be driven mad by what I say, nor they. Only know that you cannot know, and you will be the wiser."

POTTER'S WHEEL

A Potter took in his hands the clay of life and shaped it into a bubble.
He filled this bubble with lush forests perfumed with the fragrance of sighing pine
And with sparkling seas that smelled of salt and seaweed.
He worked the clay until He made hills and mountains, canyons and ravines.

He conceived of every color to fashion His bubble as He would have it.
He created the sky and willed that it morph from blue to black in a cyclical manner forever.
When he finished, the Potter washed His hands clean of the clay and smiled upon His work.
He saw that it was good.

Then there was man.
When man was born, he came to think himself a Potter.
He saw clay on his shirt and did not see anybody else around
So he took the bubble to be his own.

He scrubbed the shine out of the seas.
He suffocated the sky and siphoned it of its stars.
He levelled the hillsides in favor of homesteads.
He painted the world gray.

This is what happens when man mounts the Potter's wheel.

MY EARS

There is a thief
Somewhere out there
And he has taken
My ears.

Now I look
And all I see
Are lips moving
Soundlessly.

When I see a drummer
Striking his instrument
He may as well be
Beating a cloud.

My ears are lost
Ripped from my head
And resting in the hands
Of some villain.

Although my eyes
Have not decayed
I feel blind in the day
On account of my misunderstanding.

But in the silent night
I rest just fine
Knowing that I am just like
You.

CAPTAIN ON'S SHIP

From bow to stern, port to starboard, the *Hēilóng* was surrounded by boundless blue water. She was a moving island of red sails and black softwood that cut through the sea with an arrow's intent. Her sails were spread like dragon's wings. Creaking and groaning as she bobbed up and down swelling waves, the *Hēilóng* flew eastward in a forward manner, never slowing in the face of wind or tide.

The vast ocean glittered with the light of the sun, as did the green eyes of a young man who sat on a bench with his bare feet resting off the ship's starboard side. The young man, sporting a young beard at his jaw and a black-and-white patterned scarf around his neck, explored the clear noon sky with emerald eyes. His head was far away from him, thrust somewhere beyond the horizon, that distant, undefinable edge where blue sky met blue ocean. His only companion was his *argileh*.

The young man put the hose to his lips and inhaled. Bubbles snapped and roiled in the hookah's blue glass basin. His chest filled with smoke. He held it, then he exhaled a cloud that rose to the heavens and disappeared. He could make rings with the smoke and do other neat tricks when he had company, but today, he was alone. For some unknowable reason, the plague had taken every member of the crew but him.

SERPENTINE SHADOWS

Aristocles cannot see, for the cavern is grimly and dimly lit by dusty, dusky light. The air is humid. He feels something like fingers skittering across his back. He looks up to behold stalactites hanging from the ceiling like weavers hung from their necks. Suddenly Aristocles is met with the sight of serpentine shadows bending and twisting across the cavernous ceiling.

How many ways a serpent could kill a man! By constriction. One moment, you are hugging the creature, the next it is strangling you. By poison. One moment, you are kissing the creature, the next it is sinking its fangs into your neck. By camouflage. The snake seems friend, but its murder proves it foe.

And snakes are hungry! They eat their prey whole. Your mind, gone! Your heart, devoured! Your soul, stolen! From a spat with tigers and lions you may salvage yourself, but from a snake, there is no reprieve. Why?

Because serpentine shadows bend and twist across the cavernous ceiling. Could you tell a snake's color by its shadow? Could you count its scales? No, shadows are but shadows. They are not knowable. Invisible? No, worse! Visible, but unknown.

III

Under Caesar's watch
We are on Roman time.
Our hours are far removed
From the noise of the North.

Tired, sweating, drunk
Fleeing rain
Aware of our looming departure
But away from the noise nonetheless.

THE SWAMP

That night
The swamp was silent
But I could swear I heard fireworks
Bursting above me.

SPRINGTIME SCOTCH

A glass of scotch sweats by the fire.
Ice cubes drift silently until they melt into the amber pool.
It seems that the restless world is resting for but a night
To pay its respects.

EPILOGUE

After reading these words
The traveler felt something like candlelight in his mind.
Suddenly he recognized the hand as his own
And remembered from whence he came.

After spending but a moment in Heaven
He was sent back to earth
With a journal filled with his days
Painted in inken pictures.

He was to determine whether he was to stay or go back
For in his waking life he was on the cusp of life and death.
The journal, while confounding, was familiar in its warmth.
Indeed, the traveler saw that it was good.

He found a quill in his sleeve and wrote on the final page:

> Happy forever?
> Kindly hold off on heaven.
> One more day on earth.

ABOUT THE AUTHOR

Inspired by the pantheon of poets from the Middle East and beyond, Johnathan J. Azar abandoned his pursuit of completing a sprawling western fantasy novel in favor of simple verse. Having been born in New Jersey and raised on both coasts of the United States, Johnathan pulls from a wealth of experiences gleaned across borders to translate life into poetic form.

If you enjoyed the book, you are welcome to follow the author on Instagram @jazarauthor and leave a review on Amazon.com.

There was a time when I wondered if I was colorblind
For the colors of the trees and the leaves did not impress me.
Certainly there was something there
Something I was not seeing.

Had the sky appeared grey
I would have known that some ailment was afflicting me
But I saw the sky was blue.
I only thought it was perhaps not blue enough.

-excerpt from *16 Sleepless Nights*

Johnathan J. Azar

coming soon

Made in the USA
Middletown, DE
26 July 2019